Organic Soul

Organic Soul

Christopher Taft Kenyon

authorHOUSE®

AuthorHouse™ LLC
1663 Liberty Drive
Bloomington, IN 47403
www.authorhouse.com
Phone: 1-800-839-8640

Published by AuthorHouse   08/19/2013

ISBN: 978-1-4918-0632-6 (sc)
ISBN: 978-1-4918-0633-3 (hc)
ISBN: 978-1-4918-0631-9 (e)

Contents

Introduction

There is an essential element of nature which defies reason, logic, or science. An element which emanates from my experiences living in the majestic hills and valleys of Vermont's Green Mountains. A calling, if it were, where the working land speaks, and the wind sings, and the ever changing skies dazzle our sight with amazing color and clarity. Only when one captures the breath, the life, and the feeling of such a place which has inspired many generations by its breathtaking beauty, abundant freshness, and pastoral beckoning can one begin to understand this element.

From this element one can achieve valuable insight into more than the heart and mind of a writer, but also partake in a richer part of the fabric of life woven across fields, and lakes, and mountains always changing with the seasons. I simply share with the reader a love for poetry mostly presented in classical English sonnet style.

Further inspiration for this work will consider the role that nature plays in creating the essential element to define our life and time. I attempt to move past describing climate that only dampens or brightens daily lives to how it actually defines feelings and moods. Belonging to the Vermont experience means seeking out those treasured hollows, and stepping lightly out atop those hilly ledges, and smiling brightly at the sun and sky and water and grass. We can smile at ourselves too for all our rugged beauty.

Thankfully—partly, it must be said, thanks to the vision and sense of loyalty of generations of those who have come before us, what they have taken, and what they have left behind; this essential element collectively cherishes and preserves this unique heritage.

This essential element, I am calling.....Organic Soul.

~ Christopher Taft Kenyon

Entwined

Where sands come together at your ledges
Searching what washes on shores of treasure
Be a kiss which bumps along the edges
A place for where our love makes such pleasure

Us adrift in a tide of tranquil seas
Floating together we are meant to be
Our sails filled with the wind of offshore breeze
Searching for emerald coves with palm trees

Happen upon an island of delight
We anchor our ship inside your favor
A harbor of love all sweetness and light
Anyone whoever seeks will savor

Forever lost in time will ever find
For the sheer beauty of love be entwined

The Homeless Man

Hands thrust in pockets you walk and mutter
Thoughts alleyways of unwanted clutter
Watches rather looking at the nutter
Squinting two wild cats across the gutter

For all wrongs in life become the weeper
Cry o'er some scraps boilin' in a steeper
For not mercy of the market keeper
Safe from clutches of the dark grim reaper

Sadness that's lost in the slums and ghettos
Inspired in such classical libretto
Pours out like the smoothest amaretto
Sung an opera of such fine falsetto

Homeless and wandering drifting afloat
In a turbulent sea so sails your boat

Hold On Tightly

Countess ways your hair falls across your face
Covers briefly my gaze into your eyes
The warmth of your touch in my sweet embrace
Feels like sun parting 'tween clouds in the skies

Shimmerin' lips glossed watermelon red
Touch each nerve connected into my brain
Lovely and wet as blooms a flower bed
Shining deeper and deeper in the rain

Casting a light inside a soul once so dark
Dancing spirits in your current swirling
Going round and round in some distant arc
With no beginning or end is twirling

For only time spinning faster than light
Can break apart what we hold very tight

Tears Sank Into the Sea

Two years past since our last day together
Tears streaming from my eyes' salty rims
Heavy they sank into seas' forever
Dwelling at bottom where my heart still swims

Trapped in the gurgle of my drowning breast
My pleas for mercy screamed like greedy gulls
Chased away from mere scraps off barren nest
For even love like nature has it culls

In a world that hides its love as treasure
Lost for ages in jungles overgrown
Love only given to me in good measure
Gaining not in value what was never known

Farewell to love hid in the floating chaff
Never wash up ashore on my behalf

Loves Lightest Touch

Stars were simmering as blue as your eyes
Deep is the black night I gaze for meaning
Around goes mythic orbs of ancients rise
Align like mystical gods convening

Your flawless skin as fair shines a 'wanting
Clean as the newest ferns of spring unfurl
Fresh as the cloudless day is a dawning
Smoother then the freshest unblemished pearl

Soft my touch as pink as the setting sun
Does quiver in her slight breezy ripples
Brushed soft as the finest silk ever spun
Floating slowly around aroused nipples

Soft and so gentle is loves lightest touch
So we both enjoy ourselves very much

Feathers

Waiting with wings folded and one leg tucked
My beak buried beneath my wing no sight
Is seen sleeping so soundly head so ducked
Only darkness surrounds me in daylight

Time standing still on one stilt near shoreline
Where n'er even a slightest hint of breeze
For smooth as glass reflecting deep and fine
Causes my green and brown image to freeze

A perfect camouflage blends with a hush
Near cedars clutching in a cleft of rock
No finer detail charms an artist's brush
Nor is seen by any passing marsh hawk

Silence waits while nature blends together
Matching patterns made by perfect feathers

Let's Not Wait

Let's not wait because it doesn't matter
Casting out nets of unbridled desire
Drifting sparks of flickering fire scatter
Risks catching our two lonely hearts on fire

Soft as my fingertips run down your spine
Such loving touch belongs to another
Lying close and so helplessly supine
Our bodies entwined around each other

When only two naked souls seek cover
Safely beyond all that keeps us apart
Holding you close in my arms forever
Feeling against my chest your beating heart

Why deny those feelings we can't defend
What we want we can no longer pretend

Forty Years and Forty Nights

We should not howl loud into the hollow
Announcing all the world is doom and gloom
For time march not like death to a gallow
Waiting for the ol' volcano to plume

Forty years and forty nights an eon
Time measures deeper into space than light
Make our needs to suffer oblivion
Dulling our senses that once shone so bright

For fruits of our labor decay to dust
When the fading sky will swallow the sun
When great cracks rip across the earth's dry crust
The moment comes when darkness thus begun

Nothing safe but our spirit in the wind
Like a lonely owl keeping one eye skinned

Love in a Bottle

Tell me how long my love be cast away
Drifting hopeless in a forsaken sea
Tossed one day into the windy sea spray
Could feel utter lonely to this degree

No tides rolling back to the shores of hope
Without a chart or stars to guide my night
No rudder or compass to help me cope
Wound like a message in a bottle tight

Only glass that surrounds my fragile heart
Protects secrets written inside of it
Will be perished and smashed on rocks apart
Or gently washed on sands my Holy writ

Love perhaps lost so long ago in time
Just waiting to be found on shores sublime

Midnight Moonrise

Rising slowly above the resting woods
A shining beacon cresting o'er the hill
Less faithful is the night and worldly goods
Predations friend coming in for her kill

So great your sorcerous spirit at night
Can safely only hide in your shadow
Legends of sorrow be blamed in your sight
Places where the quail cry in the meadow

Where all speech is soft, all manners gentle
Mumbled creatures cover with hooded heads
Murmurs and chanting all transcendental
Cloaked in their long robes with darker threads

To safely watch in her shadow is odd
Precession of a perihelion god

Eyes like a Flower

Deeply your eyes color gives them a glow
Spreading such delicate bloom to the world
Shining so bright since a long time ago
Rare blossoms bursting out of damp earth hurled

Behind a great smile we greet tenderly
Shimmer when in radiant sun its sheen
With a gaze from the sky into the sea
Mine deeply blue into less deeply green

We danced like lovers in a soft caress
When drawn together once were caught within
Love was a net stronger than will I guess
When your eyes like a flower made me grin

Great is reflection of love all around
Looking at the greatest jewel ever found

Caged Inside My Bones

My delicate heart made of flesh and blood
Beating over time that the tides define
How simple each stroke arrives with a thud
A boat rocks at anchor on mooring line

Spirits in life should we love make us dance
What we crave in crest is not coherence
Seek no softness in your cold abundance
Sharing only good grace in appearance

For weak becomes our will and cold our stones
While we age growing up instead of down
A beating heart so caged inside my bones
Like a head above water will not drown

Rise gentle over cresting waves my sun
What wonders where my beating heart begun

First Signs of Spring

Those first days of spring with cheeks so ruddy
Wanting sun burns with desire winter clouds
Dares passage over meadows so muddy
Besides ice cold brook grows in misty shrouds

Sing us up vibrant song you redbreast bold
Revel a whole woods cry out Spring has Come
Wake the day alive and shake off the cold
We all know you won't let your love keep mum

Burst from the ground an iris or crocus
While we smile with our eager impatience
Who be first to show their hocus pocus
To study nature . . . is love not science

So precious a time rewinds like a clock
When the first signs of spring is all we talk

Star Sign Challenge

Aries you and me are hot to handle
Taurus you've got some hope I could wish for
Gemini so lovely burns my candle
Cancer let's share the earth we both adore

Leo like twin suns burning we're too hot
Virgo too often lift your hopes too high
Libra you give me such freedom of thought
Scorpio you're so sexy you make me sigh

Sagittarius make ourselves so strong
Capricorn let us ride the cresting wave
Aquarius don't hold me down too long
Pisces you really are charming and brave

If you love your freedom and love passion
Our love will never go out of fashion

Warlike Menace

If by chance be that creature of the wood
Searching for prey by the light of the moon
Creature of the sea be misunderstood
Traps silvery schools in shallow lagoon

Creature of the city who stalks by night
Black hoody shadows red eyes are ablaze
Indifferent to cries of fear and fright
Tears drip with blood soak darkened alleyways

Predation's eyes watches with deep peril
Boldness striking like the fangs of vipers
Coldness gazing down scope of a barrel
Steady squeezes the trigger of snipers

What about nature do we learn is evil
Schooled in survival since times primeval

Indecision

Been thinking about us a lot lately
And it's making me feel kind of a wreck
Not sure to know how to feel exactly
Just wondering how long we're going to trek

Liking each other a lot that's for sure
Can be the same as only be a friend
Who is sure things will change in the future
When we can't predict what's around the bend

Can you imagine you want more than that
Can't just not think because we think too much
Now so very torn 'cause we've arrived at
This point to make a decision as such

Love too fleeting to capture in a net
Up until the day that you and I met

Taught What's Brave

Living in a world so coarse and uncouth
When so much happiness hidden by gloom
Fighting middle ground between lies and truth
A crummy desert where no flowers bloom

For once can we all learn from happiness
War only ends when peace finally's won
Death lurking in shadows' dark ghastliness
Stops hunting our children down with a gun

Some years ago an old musket was hung
Above a mantle place of peace was sung
Never brought down and 'round a shoulder slung
Just a conversation piece for our young

War and death will dig us an early grave
So each generation be taught what's brave

Spring Meadows

At last the winters' cold spell be broken
Lest soften the foggy freeze in your grip
Givin' rise to springs and streams awoken
Castin' loose ice clingin' on rocks to slip

Return the smells of sweet earth when anew
Once molded decayed old leaves start rottin'
Burstin' fresh in new greens and shining dew
Boney limbs a forest nigh forgotten

For pure is the spring as the newborn lambs
Stand on spindly legs that freshen life brings
Melt back down riverbanks flooded ice jams
Gurgles currents fast around its bend sings

So softly now is the grass turnin' green
Wave fresh across the sunlit meadows clean

Beckoning Your Grace

Sunrise spilling light o'er a frozen lake
Still casting in deep shades of icy blue
Color back to a colder darkness make
Transparent crystals shining light its hue

For we the weary travelers of time
Casting out upon our journey will take
In the moment day beckons the sublime
A shining significance each snow flake

For only in your light does darkness shrink
Those colorless memories the nights void
Looking out from eyes of a desert sphinx
Over a sleeping world that life devoid

Shining bright every day from deep space
Giving us life by beckoning your grace

When Nothingness Matters

My frozen world becomes broken in time
Splinters of beauty does cracklin' ice bring
Those gentle clinks of a muffled wind chime
Wintered valley hear a tolling bell ring

Smokey steam rises from a running brook
Drifts lazily through a dark barren branch
Across the sleeping woods might be forsook
Iced o'er water making the earth's blood stanch

Depart these last days of winter sublime
Water turning vapor before my eyes
Restless as spirits will rise in their time
Ghostly apparitions we need surmise

Castawaya dreams imaginary
Exist either whole or fragmentary

The Coming of Spring

When in an evening of sweet quiet dream
I gaze at the stars for beauty it brings
Like a pool full of swimming minnows team
A tree full of returning songbirds that sings

My heart beat captures the raindrops that dance
A warm breeze blowing the first smell of spring
Exciting time for pairing and romance
A tree swelling proud with its new growth ring

As much in my eye as my heart grows fond
Past empyreal springs have come and gone
Auspicious another lies still beyond
Celestial horizons casts dreams on

Moments we have are like moments we share
For when everyone knows Spring's in the Air

One Winter Night

How deep resolves an achromatic moon
Shining brightest when all gloaming begets
Will comfort me late past an afternoon
Sinking deepest in silent silhouettes

Happy stars watch you pull the tides along
The rolling surf crests high her icy glaze
Come night ne'er blinds a glowing sky so strong
Nor an earth to rest in her brumal days

Winter paints a barren landscape numb
Soundless chilled by shades of snow and moon
Fleeing air heavy down from heights succumb
Spilling deeply into hushed meadows strewn

Burning into night stars shining so bright
The vast hibernal sky 'comes black and white

Angels and Dinosaurs

Swoop down come you all on your golden wings
Beckoning my pleas for your safety brings
Shining green eyes and a lizard tongue sings
With a shrilling voice from the King of Kings

No greater raptor on earth can compare
For only your fossils in earth lie bare
Waiting once again for the truth do dare
For all who knows your mystery beware

Perchance angelic image was all wrong
Art and form never human all along
In our hearts we do fear where you belong
When so much your legend became our song

Once upon a time before we humans
You were Glory, Alleluia, Amen

The Moon Will Cry

Lifting the smog beyond the city lights
Far away molecules drift out of sight
Perhaps on a vapor trail from distant flights
Crossing up strange patterns into the night

Seldom seen on western horizons far
Busy travel in the atmosphere so high
Those little trails that smoke under a star
To make one wonder just how high we fly

The train still whistles on the tracks nearby
Travelling on from city to city
The sounds of sirens always fill the sky
Like the night winds fill our hearts with pity

No reason exists for the moon will cry
Except for the fact that our earth will die

A Winter Thaw

Melt water swashes over jagged ice
Warm southern breeze lift high my piney boughs
From sleepy dens do gentle days entice
Awakened forest dweller cause to rouse

Wash warmer my face in your golden rays
Make my step bounce a little brighter yet
With nature walks the youth of early days
And all her promises of spring be met

For a winter thaw in my heart be kept
Close by this meadow's memories be born
Running down where the flood waters be swept
Washing me clean over rocks well be worn

Dances a warm winter's glowin' sunbeam
Does make my world a little less extreme

Her Soft Touch

Soft wool sweater hung loosely on her limbs
Her smile as demure as warm southern seas
Green eyes frothing in slow simmerin' swims
Rose petals falling like leaves in a breeze

Touch me, my bare heart, gently take my hand
Let me lead you in most enchantin' dance
Feet flying as drifts feathers in the wind
Soaring in spirits let's define romance

Let me smell wild lavender on your skin
Feeling, brushing silky sweet close to mine
Growing smiles each tender caressin' grin
Her soft touch . . . and my heart trembles so fine

So slowly let's dance under swirling stars
Even only in dreams . . . like sharing ours

A Winter Sunrise

In a frozen world that will never last
Those cupric blues and ferric yellow glass
An expanse of ice that is just too vast
A beautiful mosaic in nature's grasp

Such a savage wind will the sculptor show
Besides crack'd cedar fence posts in-a-row
Nature's deft display on fields of snow
As early sunrise casting shadows grow

Upside a tricklin' brook with ice so thin
No more purer water has ever been
Many fresh tracks leading back where from when
Back and forth from some softwood forest den

All around, 'who' knows most the secrets hid
Resting, a sage old owl whispers 'who' did

Icicles

Dripping icicles grow outside windows
Trapped behind these ice spears creates my cage
Sun refusing to rise makes eerie shadows
Oh short these days and long these nights we age

Quiet the sound of falling snow is mute
Spared but a slight breeze whistle in the twig
Ol' Jack Frost plucking on his off tune lute
Delighted when his captives hear his gig

A starving bird huddles on chimney peak
With fluffy feathers struggles to stay warm
A berry dangles in its tiny beak
Softly thaws in labored breath changin' form

These coldest darkest days of midwinter
'waiting for these pendent spears to splinter

Clefts in the Rock

Snow falls softly over quiet meadow
A soliloquy of stillness pervades
My floating thoughts are only an echo
Humanity hesitates and evades

A chilling cold becomes a welcomed hush
Old smile still frozen on its sightless face
Beautiful eyes once filled with tears so lush
Death welcomes all in its muted embrace

Sadly life abandons our greatest Host
A rusted barbed wire strand become our crown
Mankind becoming cold, deaf as a post
Maybe a branch a knife will whittle down

Come gather together my scattered flock
Time to stop hiding 'tween clefts in the rock

Sparkle Dreams

Glittering silver scales of a brook dace
Slivers 'neath ice of fast cold mountain streams
Moving magic shown on crystal ball's face
Shrouded in her eyes an ol' gypsy gleams

Cast adrift in the night the heavens' bring
Tiny clusters of far'way sparkly things
Voices of angels serenading sing
Floating notes reflected off golden wings

Gazing snow swept fields in moonbeams' glimmer
Tiny icicles sway from pine branch boughs
Flocking night birds silver saucers' shimmer
Up and over the drifting swirling snows

Giant unblinking golden eyes still search
When seen high upon a dead tree I perch

The Darkest Rose

Less fear scares me as dark shadows enclose
Under black shroud of a widow's blind-fold
Wearing the scent of summer's darkest rose
Blooms in a lonely field that death foretold

Eyes never drying when tears stop their flow
Nothing is as moist as the morning dew
Nor stark the color of carrion crows'
Coal black feathers turning purplish-blue

Sick in my grief was love lost in the grave
More vulnerable yet lest I ever dreamed
Continuous fear wearing down depraved
Bitterness cast from the nets unredeemed

May ones' good life be made from what's gone past
Living in sweet dreams that forever last

Mystery of Faith

The wind blew wild across the angels' wings
When all salvation is a timely thing
Hear the trumpets sounding triumphant rings
Knowing the new found Prince of Peace will bring

Across the winter seas of ice and cold
A Christmas tale be told again and known
Since today is not unlike the days of old
When spreading faith is like a seed that's blown

Only then across the cold fields of life
Within our hearts are warmed by such desire
Be known for more than just a life in strife
Wearing ecclesiastical attire

For when all you shall seek in faith conceals
Parting in clouds of mystery reveals

One Warm Glow

How warmly a'glow your fire greets me well
Just around the bend and seein' me home
Those lovely curled swirls of smoke rising s'well
Over blankets of snow's coverin' dome

For in that sweet odour born of the woods
Many a'whole days I trudged its timber
Buck sawed and stacked neat in an ol' woodshed
Countless swings of axe make me so limber

Lo' in wind drifts over meadows swagger
With these footsteps my perilous travel
Deep into snow's softin' crust I stagger
That last longest mile I dare not cavil

The fresh smell of stew in a pot simmerin'
Hanging over your soft coals shimmerin'

Mine to Blame

Those careless days as selfishness reveals
Where once all love was missing from my heart
Least solace for my fellow mans' ideals
Whose wealth only serves to set us apart

Be gentle still while my compassion swirls
Wonderful thoughts fancied soon fleeting gone
My Master would make strings of perfect pearls
As I would have no luck to happen on

Ah me, I stumble on paths well-trodden
Discarded shells glitter in my wet hands
In my pockets full of weeds well sodden
Piled up on an oceans' broken sands

Like searching into a soul I would tame
If for only my life was mine to blame

Deer Hunting

Blow hard cold gales across crumpled corn stalks
Dark skies spitting frozen granules of snow
Forcing my eyes into slits my sight blocks
Squinting for my prey down long stubble rows

Take away, just numb my other senses
Perching up on an old tree stump to sit
Cover the run for it to jump fences
My rifle held firmly in my warm mitt

Hours and hours so alone with my thoughts
For soft hush of breath inhale and depart
Like when success comes and goes casting lots
For when the moment comes with racing heart

Now my pulse quickens my blood flows fervid
Into sights my long awaited cervid

The Old Millstone

A fog rolled into the leafless hollow
Fallen and faded of glorious color
A withering rug of molding mass
Growing dark is dank November
In the midst of a life in crises
So lies swollen shut
My eyes are cried with cold
Blurry is first glimpse of snow

Now water running clean and sober
Down streambed past a boulder
Scored with ancient glacial scars
Across its smooth face bored
As stories born shiny and wet
So waits freezing still
My breath clouds into my face
Mixing with the fog that brews

And now, across a squeaking bridge
Floor of sagging wood grows moss
Hiding rot from within its mass
Cracked and rusted its paint peels
And loosens old skinny nails
So goes aging time
My heart grows weaker while
I pass the old millstone by

Boldness

Seldom following the foot path of life
A trail always winding not straight and smooth
Our sorrows like pricker bushes are rife
Many scraps and scratches we need to soothe

When caution falls in the way of our haste
When each foot step is not carefully placed
When in our boldness our trust is misplaced
When we fail to notice shoes are still laced

Always fear grows in the darkening dusk
With goals of growing from darkness to light
Civilize manners a little less brusque
Boldness becomes a little more contrite

Still hope for mankind should we slow the pace
Sometimes timidity's a safer place

My Little Leaf

You who were once so colorful and crisp
Now laying soft and limp brown with decay
Once in the gentle start of spring would wisp
A new growth bursting forth in green array

How much I watched you grow in each season
Collect from a bright sun much energy
Making me think of life with more reason
We were the center of such synergy

Now that darker skies fill with grey coldness
Whispers in the wind the winter coming
Left with yet another year of oldness
Face a hundred days of frostful numbing

Good bye my dearest friend my little leaf
You brought to me much joy in time so brief

Forever Lost

The sky a darkly growing mass of gray
"Tween streaks of setting sun make a moon rise
Feeling lost of stars aid me in my way
Lacking proof my naked eyes would devise

Forever lost of light my thoughts concealed
Cross never stood over a potter's field
Out of sight hiding all my faults congealed
Resting in silence never be appealed

Lest my mark on life be forever lost
Burnt lump of coal into a cinder made
Hurting oneself such a terrible cost
Casting salvation's light into the shade

Such as when light transfers day into night
Lacking faith no love in our hearts ignite

A Quiet Shoreline

Scarcer are days when the world feels so light
Boundless energy into dreaming eyes
Reflections of stars luminating night
When deep into dark fissures no fear lies

In my grateful walk is my head held high
Nothing in my way I take a sure stride
On a path of life that's more a journey
Across the quiet shoreline at low tide

Over sand still wet and firm my feet glide
Barely a trace to mark I have passed by
The dark sea only a hush by my side
Time moves as fast as the blink of an eye

In solitude I hear my own heart beat
With no good cause at all to drag my feet

Evening song

Lay the golden crowns a second cut made
Drying in neat rows from a twirling rake
My tractor idles in the chestnut's shade
We rest from chores taking a little break

Once long days of summer growing shorter
Less urgent the cries of the feeding young
When harvest moon enters its first quarter
Seen rising when an evening song is sung

Now a light breeze rattles the drying leaves
From the warm earth lifts an afternoon haze
Find peace 'tween a man and what he believes
Thoughtful recollections of good old days

A long slow circle back to tractor's shed
Basks in glow of setting sun, blazing red

The Storm

Whatever makes a storm so arousing
Only too happy to draw back the shades
When her long lightning bolts are carousing
Slender fingernails over open glades

When she reaches her most towering heights
With her roaring breath shaking, shuddering
When her howling wild groans in pure delight
When everyone she clasps is juddering

Shameless smile upon her seductive face
Sirens wailing after ship wrecking frights
Tempest maiden bears her name in disgrace
A very feminine name she delights

Hurricane gather over tropic sea
Into her mouth is swallowed or set free

The Mannequin

She stood so statuesque with gazing eyes
Wearing all the latest fashions with grace
Where hidden in a smile could not disguise
Any meaning from her suggestive face

Mona Lisa eye lashes in fashion
Skin white as finest alabaster clay
Hair changing colors as leaves in season
Her style was always the style for the day

Perked and prized inside of her gilded cage
Passerby fancied her perfecting shapes
Rivaling as best ancient goddess stage
Piety once dressed in immortal drapes

The street lights reflecting her long white gloves
Ideal is . . . is the mannequin who loves

Castaway on the Moon

Blackbirds in flight over a restless sea
Cloudy days casting dark feelings appall
Tossed high like driftwood beyond foaming scree
Sadness shadows my door once and for all

Casting no hope deep in a storm's cold eye
No warmth is found in a coat so shoddy
Lady luck laughs with each roll of the die
Spins her web up and over my body

Never tasted such fear entombed within
Confined inside space so soft and silky
Where darkness increases every spin
In a galaxy defined as milky

A time capsule not to open too soon
Might as well be castaway on the moon

Wisdom in the Woods

Dozen old maple trees equally spaced
Seemingly planted down a lost dirt road
Perhaps on edge of forgotten field traced
No longer any memories bestowed

I imagine once stood an old farmhouse
Just a pile of jagged and broken stone
In a rusted pail now home for a mouse
Secrets 'neath a canopy overgrown

May a forest reclaim old settled lands
No boundaries left mark once was surveyed
Gone too is the presence of working hands
Be still listen to warblers serenade

Mysteries over years as time marches on
A long row of old maples I now gaze upon

Reflections in Nature

With sadness looking around each corner
Blurry eyes still searching for some lost hope
Betrayed by death will become its mourner
Always wondering how we'll ever cope

Floating in a small stream the ducks will graze
Moving slowing around each bending reed
Drifting down the shoreline shifting our gaze
Silently watching lonely hunger feed

Lost in confines of this most peaceful place
Reflections filled in nature's paradise
Each tender stalk ripples its state of grace
Refreshing thoughts in a clear pool advise

Nature's peace given on these restless days
Abundantly found in sun's setting rays

Eyes So Icy Blue

Time spreads apart many crests of a wave
Flow in cadence falling on sandy shores
Wash away any trace our souls to save
Even our footprints vanish mine and yours

Eyes shine like liquid stars so icy blue
Blind almost so pale in color make ghosts
Bumps up against darkness' glittering hue
Where deep green sea meet at the coasts

Forever drowned in a dream when each breath
A stench of decay mists into my breast
That what leaves behind after cheating death
Through rocky portals swirl a life compressed

A dank stormy night face a mighty sea
When gulls are crying and laughing at me

Under Your Spell

Casual as drifting stars spark at night
Many thoughts for us floating over time
Hoping at long last for love to ignite
Ever guiding light towards a goal I climb

Lost now how many days will pass us by
When neither one of us dare take a chance
Waiting for more lonesome tears to drip dry
Will wash away the meaning of romance

Sadly even starry nights grow longer
Offer gladness yet we still feel glummer
What could make my dreams for you feel stronger
Cast in doubt a shadow moon midsummer

Please pardon me this most serious blunder
It must only be your spell I'm under

Some Soft Rain

A soft mood dampens hanging branches with rain
Grey billowy storm clouds bump against sky
Dripping off eaves wetting dark barn boards stain
Like artists' pallet fill a weather eye

Long may your soft drips make me feel lonely
Tearful drops running down my window pane
Look out from blurry eyes will clear only
Even to fix my poor visceral brain

Often needed quiet moments perplexed
Thinking deeply about how things are swept
Many choices not found in sacred text
A place where no easy answers are kept

Only life and love will wash clean from lust
For if we are just a machine we'd rust

Odontoceti

Hiding low my deep voice in depth of sound
More vocal my watery world than yours
Many miles in distance my presence found
Yet not far from the glimmering Azores

Large at birth swimming a winnowing sea
Transiting as I do from pole to pole
Roams vast a spirit for remaining free
Carefree I go shimmering shoal to shoal

Alive with such hope for life eternal
So much older now and so much wiser
Fills a legend from a sailor's journal
My famous name now flows like a geyser

Relate to Jonah tales of Israel
Be watchful for spirit of Ishmael

Lasting Beauty

Flourishing from a parched earth without hope
Plastic red rose fading pink on dark grave
Thrown down an overgrown river bank slope
Worthless lifeless object no need to save

A moment once for a sad occasion shared
Arranged so neatly in a Styrofoam base
Such as a life where pain was never spared
Or cut bleeding from thorns in any case

Was a life never dried and blown to dust
When many frequent rains had come to pass
Growing tall and straight from the earth's soft crust
As tender as blades of new velvet grass

Life is like light being born so must pass
Stained glass windows through shards of broken glass

Paddling Paradise

Full summer sun over water edges
Shove away kayak from shore at Mac's Bend
Down river past the towering sedges
A story about worlds that never end

Any splendor more worthy to relish
When nature appears right before your eyes
Is a wonderful life to embellish
Better than anything minds will devise

Such is red fox trotting down the shoreline
Hunting in search of some prey to come by
Fiercely two eyes a predator combine
With such cunning and skill can under lie

My kayak on the water drifting by
Will always simply give me the glad eye

Dandelion

How great you are the mighty lion's tooth
Emerging through the mottled winter kill
Bursts into life so many blooms of youth
Lying your yellow carpet down the rill

In these longer hours for daylight to pass
Just below the ridge running wild with ease
Happens at once the snowdrift melts alas
Change mindless dullards into swarming bees

A springtime welcome sign like no other
Gives up sweet nector make hives of honey
Such a gift to give our earthly mother
Greater your gold than glitter of money

When your aging blooms turn to hollow globes
Watching wind blow your parachuted robes

Broken Ladder

Cautiously I walk night hours on mean street
Pitbull stretched on chains waiting to attack
Courthouse stands behind reinforced concrete
Reminders of life we want to take back

Sirens erupt and shatter peaceful night
Screeching tires lay down rubber's foolish grin
An old lady pulls down her shades in fright
Lonely souls wait for darkness to begin

Loud are idle youth that travel in packs
Pretend to be brave and laughing out loud
Carelessly roaming and crossing wrong tracks
A fight breaks out inside a huddled crowd

Ends to vulgarity is violence
When jobless youth are losing innocence

Forest Dweller

Have fear my little mythical creatures
Found running and making wild in the woods
Paint a magical pole of strange features
Nearby the mound of your ancestor 'hoods

Like green moss crawling along a dark wave
Into a pleasant valley rich in depth
Wild flowers clinging to mouth of cave
Glancing behind into a dark woods breadth

You only spoke to me on sunny days
Playfully throwing little sticks and stones
Laughing and hiding from hot sunny rays
By making all those strange noises unknown

Fear cast the shadow of an old grey bird
One dark screech rest your soul be ever heard

Close Encounters

Seldom do my thoughts roam so running wild
With such passion that lights my heart on fire
When you strolled by me your sweet smile beguiled
Nothing could stop the heat of my desire

Help me if you believe I cannot hide
There's no chance to escape your lovely eyes
Exists any place for more truth to confide
Without running away with deceit and lies

Life becomes like a universe divides
Step away from its center a distance
What will cause us an event to collide
Is plotting a course of least resistance

So next time you think we don't stand a chance
Remember what turns love into romance

Love Interview

Why do I hide my greatest love from you
To only blend in with the grass that grows
Crowded by weeds when only neglect grew
Simply by now who really cares or knows

What creates love is life's greatest magnate
When it's really me you wanted to know
When attraction never becomes stagnant
Just another seed you wanted to sow

So show me a face so I may know you
Be grateful in your nourishment and care
Life is not competing in some game show
For silly people in the world to share

Only seek what you solely want to share
Only enough for you to want to care

The Raffish Ruffians

Life's a party held for your good measure
For spoiled rotten brats who lives with ease
Still hoping to steal more family treasure
Picking fruits from a basket as you please

What causes all you lost souls to suffer
Existing in a world so filled with strife
Can you think of any streets much tougher
With people who don't value their own life

Once happy playgrounds now filled with anger
Ruled by bully gangs looking for some fights
Like watching neon signs flash with danger
With sirens and strobing red and blue lights

Stumbling home drunk after dark so raffish
Can be so proud of the life you lavish

Meadow Night

Seconds wait on a clock awakening
Some hours will end before my night is done
Working, thinking, just making a living
Rest only comes with my mind on the run

Faraway coyotes howling their jive
Rest does not come as slow moon arises
Waiting, watching, trying to stay alive
Care only takes what caution surmises

A cry in the wild followed by silence
Hungry predacious eyes gleam in the night
Resting, sleeping, now safely in my trance
Time is quiescence 'till day comes to light

Everything is moving and staying still
A newborn calf a'tasting nimble will

Rule of Thumb

Only drops of sweat beating off my brow
On long simmering days of summer heat
Won't fail a heart in content up to now
Withers away my spirits in defeat

Bucket by bucket from a well running dry
Carefully spilt onto each tender plant
Soaks into the earth must give it a try
Enough to hold on be ever so scant

Hope is forecast looks promising for rain
Back to the fields with a hoe in my hand
Pulling more weeds and fertilize again
Cause now is the time to make a firm stand

Success or failure when rains at last come
Counts how you measure with a rule of thumb

Mountain Glory

A fallen tree spans o'er a gurgling brook
A shiny creature 'neath streaks rainbow hue
Around swirling eddies finds a safe nook
Hiding in the foam and froth oozing through

Each careful step light on feet I approach
My huddled form crawling down on all fours
Closer and closer as I dare to encroach
Cautious for a shadow stay on the shores

Now with a much practiced flip of the wrist
Cast away line tied to bright feathered fly
In an instant jerks its head with a twist
My line goes taut in the blink of an eye

Quickly I reel in towards the closest shore
A fabled mountain brook trout I came for

Rain Dancing

Gather the children for our hope rescinds
Counter greed driving the land into thirst
Watch anger swirl like lies into hot winds
While resentment curls the crops of the cursed

When will this terrible drought ever end
That makes a savage spirit parched and dry
Move fast little feet a message to send
As caked and cracked mud will make the land die

Form a circle of hope and play your flutes
Gently tap with love from all those soft soles
Inside your circle ring of dancing boots
A deep oasis of peace in your souls

Tap a beat to Great Gitche Manitou
Bring the rain again with some truth to sow

Spirit Walking

When walking aimless down an old dirt road
My restless soul drifts away like a cloud
Desperate to lighten my weary load
Fleeing troubled world of the disavowed

Afloat the birdsong and chirping crickets
Weaker and stronger coming and going
Sweet berries growing wild in the thickets
Gently leaves rattle in a breeze blowing

Castaway my soul drifts from its mooring
Not aided by some confined moving hull
Such freedom won is very alluring
Escaping vagrant thoughts outside my skull

A slow and quiet journey down this road
Where my spirit floats and lightens my load

Two Worlds

Do not be fooled by this silly fool's grin
How my day went don't know where to begin
Like hiding how hopeless I feel within
Please pour me a glass of tonic and gin

Unfold my cramped arms from across my chest
Been all day since I took a real deep breath
Work shakes me up get all fizzy when stressed
Sometimes my life is like dancing with death

At last I cross through the portal of home
It's time to check my baggage at the door
Always good to hear a hearty 'welcome'
Such simple greeting is hard to ignore

Not keeping apart two worlds is a sin
Where one leaves off let another begin

Border War

A thousand steps walking a crooked fence
Meanders across a craggy rock strewn field
This boundary only makes little sense
A clumsy border to keep one's eyes peeled

Tufts of grass ring the badly cratered ground
Jagged shards of twisted steel lie in rust
Only a monstrous waste of life be found
Threads in between the warring tribes of trust

If only glory could walk a fabled past
Across a barbed and razor sharpened wire
Would anyone give hope for peace to last
A much better reason for a cease fire

When borders cease to create a barrier
Indeed the whole world becomes merrier

Back to Earth

So fair and fickle as a full grown child
Youth is captured in your radiant smile
A name you chose to become more styled
Is masking what you've been known for a while

When fame and fortune replacing your soul
Is not something you ever consider
Why wonder why life is out of control
When you sell life to the highest bidder

The limelight glows on the stage you enter
For turning back is out of the question
A spotlight shines on you front and center
And accounts for your manic depression

When fame sets you apart from the masses
Time to take off those rose colored glasses

Golden Sunset

Golden sunset behind towering trees
Shining on little leaves with rustic hues
Feeling on my face a river of breeze
Sitting on shoreline watching light diffuse

Each leaf but a small reflection of thought
Making such beauty right before my eyes
So teach me good world all I can be taught
Painting these swirling colors in the skies

Sitting to watch and wonder how clever
What each day makes shall be its lasting mark
Content as a smile goes on forever
Such as daylights final minute of arc

What grander than life painting leaves on fire
That golden sunset when daylight expire

Some Shining Love

Sometimes I think for no better reason
Than a mood to create love is casting
So cycles of life and the four seasons
Are always changing and everlasting

So when our golden dreams go up in smoke
Many lonely nights become filled with fears
Bless those sylvan shadows their broader stroke
Matte dull the sadness flowing out in tears

Hardly ever once when we were younger
So much time alone in this face was carved
Where no wrinkles ever knew such hunger
Skin sagging off yellow bones feeling starved

Truly only dullness lacks fo' luster
So be all the light that love can muster

Some Summer Eve

Take a beachside stroll on a starlit night
Under canopy of a silver moon
Walking along with your eyes gleaming bright
Thinking of a good harvest coming soon

Given to me these long days of summer
When many fragrant flowers fill the fields
All around the boathouse lights will hummer
Thousands of hungry moths with shiny shields

Gently the tall grasses bend and quiver
Rolling along like waves of golden grain
Standing near sparkling waters deliver
Brightly burning fires ringed in stones remain

Wonder a warm night just to sit and gaze
For all the beauty of life does amaze

Sweet Summer Rain

Now many hot days and dry earth repeat
Lost in a cloud of dust on a dirt road
When newly planted crops wilt in sun's heat
The spring up in my meadow rarely flowed

When all hard work slows to barely a crawl
Even the panting fox gives up his chase
Clever rabbit stares like a sawdust doll
A little relieved for some breathing space

Then a cool breeze blows from the north-northwest
Gathering clouds rise in darkening dusk
A hawk circles three times around its nest
Long awaited raindrops appear so brusque

For the drought would end after a fortnight
Much do farmers dance with giddy delight

Penniless Bench

With a broken body and broken mind
Hobbles crippled into the park to sit
Daily watch feeding some crumbled old bread rinds
To a few friendly birds he'd never quit

Tattered clothing old and out of fashion
A rough, hard weathered look upon his face
His are endless days without much passion
While Passersby's glance away in disgrace

Long ago wounded and now most forgetful
His body wrecked with the passing of time
A great victory no less merciful
Listen every noon the church bells still chime

Pitiful sight whose clothes have such a stench
Sits a great hero on Penniless Bench

Love's Fool

Watch and wait things will always get hotter
Sooner or later love will turn around
What grass really grows greener and wetter
Grass over the fence or all over town

What can be argued in and of itself
Stop, think about what you already know
To even change one thing about myself
Is when your love is only 'just for show'

Searching halfway across the universe
Hoping to find what was already found
How can anyone of us just converse
When speaking faster than the speed of sound

When all you can say is all you just heard
Better believe you are being absurd

Hidden World

Hiding in tall grasses a world unseen
Pass creatures over and under the ground
Only visible to sight very keen
In the slightest indentation or mound

So life exists which we're barely aware
No appreciation or knowledge gains
A living world as if not even there
Under marching feet which only disdains

Clever creation works in small places
Against unconscious attempts to destroy
Look closely again at Queen Anne's laces
Many creatures living there to enjoy

Down the dark tunnels dug in the grasses
On hands and knees . . .magnifying glasses

Celestial Lover

Dreamy goddess of distance and romance
Far beyond my lonely world do you reign
In fields of wild flowers watch floating dance
Your flowing headdress made of daisy chain

Long days working in fields of dusty haze
A farmer's life tilling the good brown earth
At first evening star I rest and will gaze
Fruits of my labor bring to you such mirth

Every sunrise I greet with great pleasure
Your graceful perfections smile down on me
Thankful each season's for fullest measure
Smile back into your soft radiant eyes

Great Ceres make multiple my hay bales
Run wild the foxes with flaming tails

Green-Eyed Monsters

Will there ever be some good remedy
For malaria makes the skin jaundice
But perhaps is the world's worst malady
Making roots in the soils of avarice

There really can be no admiration
Only sharpened tongues wave covetously
Cutting to ribbons with insinuation
Hissing in the language of jealousy

What an unpleasant sight to begrudge
Someone else with a vile spit of envy
Such hideous eyes made narrow judge
Hides in a lair of poison ivy

Crawl on your belly for your deadly sin
Lowly green-eyed serpent living within

Remember Gram

I think of an apple-cheeked old lady
Skin as smooth and pink as any schoolgirl
Home cooking that cure any malady
A black straw sailor's hat and string of pearls

Doing dishes always with apron slung
No words of gossip from your lips would sling
Pointing out our shortcomings terse words flung
But ready chuckle took away their sting

You hated flies above all things unclean
A steady fly swatter was your scepter
Angels best keep their wing feathers well preened
And keep the pearly gates all aglitter

Might the path leading away from the past
Be always swept clean right after breakfast

Crèche of Eiders

Old rock cliffs trying to stop a sea that vaults
Like little flowers cling to a craggy cleft
Only a few feet from spraying sea salts
With such brutal force heaves the tidal heft

Leeward to all of the pounding surf rests
Just barely inside the Cape's jutting shoals
A small colony of fat eiders nests
Overfilled with fish taking waddled strolls

Everywhere the sound of the crashing sea
Filling the air with nature's symphony
I listen humbled to lesser degree
As land and sea pops in disharmony

Standing at the edge of earth's palisades
Thinking of the tales of King Orodes

Down East Coasters

Now the ox carts drove off the loading pier
Newly emptied of their stacks of cord wood
Into schooners the first loads of the year
Just waiting 'a chance' to sail and make good

South to Boston would the Coasters make runs
Fair winds not beat to windward shall they go
Sailing vessels with loads more than sixty tons
Hulls not too tight o'er shoals do the tides flow

A day's ration of rum passed among hands
More brought back with stores from city docks
And from tavern to tavern across the lands
Replenish for the winter all new stocks

Back and forth shouts the sailors still wigging
Dreamily watch the clouds drift by the rigging

Grass Widow

She would never really own her own place
Even life was not always hers at times
To end and die so slowly in disgrace
A sinner of her time and lowly crimes

The night she died in a cold driving rain
A village outcast for bringing such shame
While her lover knew not her numbing pain
To him she was just some kind of fair game

Many years have passed and weathered her stone
Set aside off the path where others passed
Beneath the wild grass is hid overgrown
The name of a poor and forgotten lass

The most perfect wild rose in the meadow
Over the grave of the young grass widow

The Wishing Pool

Bottom of pool in the fountain glimmers
Many coins tossed with such longing wishes
Some desperation when bad love simmers
So any wish come true so astonishes

Where have all the giggling children gone
Over many years and wishes ago
Even a lonely dream to chance upon
Give a chance to believe is 'quid pro quo'

So reach deep inside your pocket pants
Lift out a coin for at least romance
Maybe see whatever luck it grants
A smile to wear is worth the chance

As coin leaves your hand to join the cache
Into the mysterious pool it will splash

Catawampous

Flowing like raw sewage in the gutter
Becomes the opulence of your success
The gated walls on your hilltops shutter
Out any sight the very souls you oppress

What is born from privilege will always rest
When more work needs to be done for others
So many struggle to survive their best
Downwind from your fire a smoke smothers

Somehow always the rich will gain in wealth
Carelessly grows the weeds of Olympus
Stench of poverty is not very stealth
In the air chawers some catawampous

Unguided ungracious acts of meanness
Make for many a poor life meaningless

Simple Country Life

Long in sunny hollow does grass grown green
Watching apple blossoms fall in the breeze
Slowly drifting past are clouds so serene
Great time to daydream or do as you please

Out behind the yellow farmhouse finds you
Hanging all our fresh washed clothes on a line
Nothing better can a warm spring sun do
Make any linens fresher or smell so fine

Living in the fair countryside immune
Far away from the city's smog and noise
Smelling sweet fragrance when wild flowers bloom
Is something very few of us enjoys

How great it makes a simple country life
A peaceful place for a man and his wife

Melodia Celeste

In soft glowing moonbeams our spirits dance
I feel you watch me from a higher place
Closing my eye lids into a deep trance
Feel your sweet gentle spirit touch my face

How kind and gentle a heart always true
Blue eyes will glow and flaxen hair will wave
What centuries of time love ne'er knew
Will ever be held fast inside a grave

So when a wind gently caress my cheeks
I feel your spirit tender touch my lips
So precious is a loss a love still seeks
Not measured in a cup that always drips

A name on stone says simply Calista
Old tune playing 'melodia celeste'

Winged Lovers

Passion escapes on newly emerged wings
Take flight dear lover to heights far above
Above dull drabby dampness water brings
Stay with me awhile we twitter with love

Rest not weary souls for our lives are short
Leave all your worries with discarded ghost
Our flight will become our grandest consort
So before we fall let's make it the most

Who shall dare decry such flights immortal
Trudging away slow strides in lakes below
Far away sky a pleasurable portal
For once, and only once just let it go

Life we cherish is not for the taking
For all the more happier love making

Fractured

How deep the faults lie under our feet
Across many vast expanses of time
Lost for eternity is obsolete
Never to recall lest the old bell chime

A heart beats strong and smooth to its core
Unfaltered by any unfaithful crevasse
If faith could hold us together evermore
There'd be no fear for love to perisse

Alas! Like earth love has no window
For such force we can never foresee
So precious is time that fate foreshadow
Negating science all its repartee

Wisely know in age of uncertainty
Only love can last an eternity

Spring Pastures

Last cow into the barn is called "Skinny"
Chewing tufts of green grass near the fence post
A whole herd mooing bovine hootenanny
Waiting a turn for the milking parlor

Lush spring meadows growing moist new grasses
Yellow meadowlarks found hovering high
Something special about them blue irises
Growing down by gurgling brook nearby

All around apple blossoms in a buzz
The honey bees come to and fro the hive
What a sight to see what all nature does
Even when those barn swallows take a dive

Spring is a wonderful and active place
When all of nature is a state of grace

Floating Driftwood

Some moments when I look at you funny
A most demure smile spreads across your face
Daintily laugh and mumble "Oh Honey"
When I am serious you think it's child's play

Ok! Ok! Now what have I to say
No words can describe feelings can't confess
Lacking sincerity just fade away
So many thoughts are lost while we digress

Away, my words flee from you in a flood
Our confusion wasted like energy
Causing friendship become stuck in the mud
While taking classes in "Dramaturgy"

What if my thoughts were ever understood
Instead of floating around like driftwood

Calista

Is your name now just barely legible
So carefully etched on flaking grey stone
A name that became so adorable
In an old field now largely overgrown

Across the generations, across time
Standing near your grave and your resting soul
Mournful eye spies wildflowers sublime
A beautiful spring sky above a knoll

Every year since first I found your name
While out hunting turkeys in this old field
In remembrance to only you became
A name exists like no other revealed

The name of a woman called Calista
A name that still holds so much charisma

Knight of Gimmemoor

In past fabled lands did noblemen rob
The humble peasants of their flocks of sheep
Stealthily at night rode the black masked mob
On dark stallions while the village did sleep

Searching the bottomland of Gimmemoor
Led by a young knight this den of thieves
Caught in the act with such deeds so impure
Shamefully such nobility conceives

Leading the charge in gallivanting style
Weapons drawn against men cut down to shreds
The brave people fought back once in a while
As commoners conquered the purebreds

Such as the past is the present my friend
Be not fooled when high and mighty pretend

The Ghost of Kissing Bridge

Appearing at a distance I see you standing
many years dressed out of fashion, still watching me
with your golden long hair and green woolen tunic

Myself a child walking home on a rainy day
shadow clouds moving fast across my mirrored path
many years dressed out of fashion, still watching me

Close by the covered bridge crossing a swollen creek
you are standing, slowly, turning a pale white cheek
shadow clouds moving fast across my mirrored path

My eyes only stare a second but cannot stay
something stirs me in disbelief to gaze away
you are standing, slowly, turning a pale white cheek

With new courage looking back to where you once stood
may the legend of kissing bridge be understood
something stirs me in disbelief to gaze away

Whenever such a love so great in life is lost
appearing at a distance I see you standing
May the legend of kissing bridge be understood
with your golden long hair and green woolen tunic

Loss

So much is loss in a dream awoken
Fading away like little torn swatches
Trying to recall her soft words spoken
A Dali painting of melting watches

Sadly how thoughts mired into the lonely
As the morning sun wisps away her face
In thin air escapes my one and only
Vanishes as consciousness takes its place

Me alone into this world to survive
Being torn away from her flesh and blood
As only happens when death does deprive
Feelings washed away in a rising flood

A good memory better than a dream
Is what only the spirit can redeem

Fountain in the Park

A fountain in the park where lovers gather
past her naked copper breasts, a goddess gazes
This is the place where songbirds blather

The apple blossoms drop down one by one
soft breeze flutters, stops, then picks up again
past her naked copper breasts, a goddess gazes

under the falling water, down her wings, drips
making little splashes like rainbow raindrops
soft breeze flutters, stops, then picks up again

blowing our hair, across our faces, hiding
smiles we share, when no words can describe
making little splashes like rainbow raindrops

across the fountain in a dazzling dance
we gaze at love, at life, at romance
smiles we share, when no words can describe

those moments dearest to our hearts
A fountain in the park where lovers gather
we gaze at love, at life, at romance
This is the place where songbirds blather

Little Wild Rose

Little wild rose growing in the meadow
Not like any such flower ever grown
Rare as only nature can foreshadow
Beauty is only beauty of one's own

May I find a flower like a wild rose
Who really must be standing out alone
Her scent such sweet perfume under my nose
Her eyes be brilliant as a precious stone

Care not for me a lass like all the same
Careful cultured perfection lacking soul
Rather a little less like some Grande dame
Just more cheerful and happy on the whole

Love waits for someone precious I am told
And a wild rose be neither bought nor sold

Portals of Time

Passing through all these portals over time
Lying on the edge of consciousness rift
Swaying back and forth between stars we climb
To the center where both our souls will drift

Please give me back what will not float away
Become trapped in rings that orbit my core
Like holding a match to papier-mâché
Cannon shots through sails of a 'man-at-war'

Once again my dreams be set free at sea
Cause only there separates day from night
Sets our senses to some highest degree
The sunrise and sets in sweetness and light

That all these portals of time passing through
Make many days blessed for me and you

Growing Storm

Walking down by seashore's dawning light
Casting a pink sunrise over gulls in flight
Far in distance from shore a ship sails
Roundin' long harbor buoys painted white

Standing alone my feet dug into sand
Searching some meaning to understand
Surf rolling on over the jutting shales
The sea an endless force upon the land

A world so large around my tiny form
Dark clouds announce a growing storm
Fish pushed up by the rising swales
Screeching now the gulls begin to swarm

Broken Home

Windows all broken many years ago
Old rusted roof saddled between gables
Overgrown and bending limbs hanging low
High grass is growing wild by the stables

No handle found on the old water pump
Paint is peeling off like paper birch bark
Old oil cans litter rusted rubbish dump
The whole place is just waiting for a spark

Long ago an old man died with no heirs
And nobody showed up to stake a claim
Now has sit sixty years with no repairs
Time has all but forgot the family name

A house is just a house and not a home
When within its walls no families roam

My Meadow Bright

My ephemeral lonely wood anemone
So delicate and satin soft your face
Playfully bounce a dance of Gemini
Fill my woodland home with a state of grace

How bright is your white in the dawning light
When those first golden sunrays adorn you
Making me cheer my morning meadow bright
When walking down the old path passing through

Growing sun cause another season past
Too soon your lovely face will fade to pink
Forever etched in mind your image last
Each early spring cause me to catch a wink

Sometimes beauty last only a few days
Like the vernal flowers nature displays

Memento Mori

Out of the earth came sensational fire
Red hot glowing charred embers under me
Careful to walk in such fiery mire
Cautious about burns in the third degree

Standing still over the cauldron's hot edge
I watch smoke pillaring high overhead
Raising my arms to pray and make my pledge
What to do when I see the dragon's head

Enchanted lands beyond mythical lore
Keeping a child listening in a trance
Imagination to brace oneself for
Mighty as St George with his golden lance

The fun and thrill of those bedtime stories
When chivalry was "Memento Mori"

Beach of Understanding

Sitting on the shore time almost stands still
A cloudless sky filled with nothing but blue
A single eye looks down the heron's bill
An ancient hunting style so tried and true

Great lazy gulls fly on wings so silent
Minnows in shallows of tranquility
Everywhere is rest at peace not violent
How does one measure such gentility

Even in nature are moments of rest
Think how mankind would do well to study
Does ceaseless untiring nature bequest
Counting time off from carnage so bloody

Even so, none the less, notwithstanding
Sits still on a beach of understanding

Restless Wind

A warm summer night for a little sail
Watching golden sunsets awash in red
A lonely gull lights on the starboard rail
With gentle curiosity wings still spread

Whitecaps rolling a wake rippled with foam
Steady while our bow cuts across the waves
Tacking now we turn abreast pressing home
One final reach let's hope the wind behaves

My father's hand holds steady the tiller
I watch smoke rising off his Billiard pipe
Coming into the wind was a thriller
Grabbing the mooring line on the first swipe

Now many of a 'summers come and gone
Many restless winds to keep an eye on

Ice Age

Ten thousand years ago trapped in the ice
Tiny bubbles of air frozen don't move
Slow moving mountains of ice cut and slice
Scoring bedrock with many a deep groove

Great whales ruled the oceans of ages past
Woolly Mammoths thundered over the plains
Where primitive man during this time massed
Huddled in caves learns how fire maintains

The ice is almost gone as glaciers melt
And the last of the great bears appear doomed
How the little creature called man is knelt
Hovels while the dying embers consume

Our progression is not measured in time
For what we do to our earth is a crime

The Backwoods

Wandering logging trail follows the stream
Cutting through and around a rocky ledge
In the deep woods sounds a melodic theme
Soft wind gently brush past every sedge

Water is running high as snowpack's melt
Washing clean banks of decaying rubble
Sunlight through empty canopy is felt
Peacefully feels far from all my trouble

Only the rush of wind and waves moves
Swaying metronome of natural rhythm
Restoring a spirit which so approves
Under halos of a waterfall prism

Taking a walk into another time
Transposing concrete into the sublime

Appalachian Morning

Almost lost but for light of high moon
Reflects a sun still shining over sea
Drifting away dreams that vanish too soon
Fog burning off to a lesser degree

Silence is stillness in an early spring
A time when even the night creatures rest
Calming hours before the daylight bring
Gently the first breeze will blow north by west

Solitude spreads evenly like the dew
Quietly above does the mountain watch
Searching like eyes of a baby raptor
Gazing from a nest in its hidden notch

Soon a most beautiful sunrise will stun
Awakening all where life has begun

Love Child

A world unknown since the dawn of ages
Lays deep in the hearts of the truly wise
The truth revealed only in small stages
Perfection approached over swirling lies

What's more to love to surrender oneself
Falling into the arms of another
No piercing arrows of a little elf
For passion's fire despair will soon smother

Simple truth reflected in our nature
We must nourish a gentle loving race
A baby will cling to life we nurture
A time hard for our memory to trace

The value of every human life
Is equal in a world devoid of strife

Darkest Star

Light from the darkest star shining on me
Travelling from blackest regions of space
Caught like the deepest creature in the sea
Wriggles in your net humble, needing grace

No longer hidden as I twist and turn
Shimmering light on my defenseless core
Trapped hopeless in the point of no return
Brings to surface what I try to ignore

There's no escaping great moments of truth
Twisting and turning my head in disgrace
Swimming in lies is really quite uncouth
When dimmest star light still shines on my face

Close to creation is found in the heart
Good love always sustains from the start

Spring Showers

Smell the first fallen rain like broken chalk
Dampening odors of decaying rot
Freshening air I breathe out on a walk
Deeply caught up in such collective thought

Watch as steam rises off the new plowed field
Puddles will soon form turning dust to clay
Stand under canopy wood's edge will shield
Rest a little while from the working day

Spring showers come quickly and soon pass by
A moment of silence across the land
Not even the high shrill of songbirds' cry
Solitude spreads that I don't understand

Peacefulness found in an early spring rain
Will repeat itself again and again

What Matters

What really matters in this world you ask
Look at the pond where the sunsets shimmer
Sitting on the shore where to lay and bask
Watching all the gorgeous color glimmer

Hike up past the forest filled with softwood
Where puffy white clouds drift just overhead
To almost reach up and touch where I stood
Way above where my quiet valley spread

The wind and sun and stars know who you are
As time will stand aside and let you pass
Await the end of night for morning star
Marvel at the beauty of old sea glass

Subtle greatness of life lies everywhere
By walking away from vanity fair

Lussica

Her eyes glowing green with devilish gleam
Tilting her head obeying master's calls
Beware her stare cuts like a laser beam
Her thick raven hair around her face falls

She howls like the wind on a stormy night
Prowling the dark shadows on the back streets
Drifting like a ghost in and out of sight
Desires a man's soul like a cut of meat

Utter her name will cause such fear to rise
So evil her ways are hard to believe
What only a lonely heart can surmise
Many men of the night she will deceive

So when you go out on a one-night fling
Take greatest care to know what she might bring

Grass Turning Green

Finding those first blades of grass turning green
Cheering spring sun strong on southern slopes
Little streams filled of snowmelt runs so clean
Bring feelings we have that govern our hopes

Long before the first swelling buds open
On my face feeling warmth of a fresh breeze
When the color of a blue sky deepen
With a promise this season guarantees

Walk with me down past those tattered cattails
Coming apart like old cushion pillows
Tossing out the last decaying hay bales
Where the smoke from an old grass fire billows

When an end of old winter scene does make
Clumps of dead grass clog the combs on my rake

Orchid of My Love

Please seduce me as I am growing wild
Hanging down from canopy of jungle
Born with love is freedom's natural child
Rid me of all your corporate fungal

Please treat me not too cold and not too wet
I need your glowing heat and steamy love
Give me more a few nights in dripping sweat
With your love wild passion undreamed of

Sensually touching your skin pacifies
Embroidered silk on a empress's dress
So rich your violet color amethyst
Good virtue transforming delicate stone

Searching over the world for charming grace
I long to fall into your sweet embrace

Old Hard'ack Hill

Barren and worn down do the trails still snake
Wind through the woods topping old Hard'ack hill
Where once seashores stood unearthed clamshells break
Reborn from the frost down a hillside spill

Give me an hour or give me a whole day
Sit on a rock left from past glacial till
Sunup to sundown many shadows play
High above heard cry is a hawk's high shrill

A view from ledges of valley below
Rocky island surrounded by dry land
A boyhood dream with a desire to know
Leads back to this place again and again

A place where ancient Native spirits roam
Where nature abounds, this place I call home

Love's Glowing Ember

Like a bright glowing ember ever flew
Hit my heart and started a fire burning
So there would be no getting over you
Such as me only a fool needs learning

I can't believe some dreams I never knew
For all they'd do keeps me sadly yearning
For only such a heart that feels so blue
Harden as stone on a cold day turning

Love can only promise what it can't keep
Always leaving my consciousness churning
Then many a nights when there is no sleep
A phantom spirit that keeps returning

Spare no love that can never go away
That leaves me alone to turn old and gray

Smoke In Marrs Hollow

Rise to the morn in my hollow I will
Awake and awash my face from all sleep
When sunrise tops the ridge o'er East Hill
Hear the gentle sound of a frog's first peep

Casually I make some thoughts for the day
Chore list as long as a shadow in spring
Feeding cows in barn a few bales of hay
Ride to the woods and hear early birds sing

Not just late winter does mud season start
Buckets they hang from a tree by a tap
Sugaring begins first full moon in March
Drip drip they fill with a maple's sweet sap

The smoke will rise from the hot boiling pan
Maple syrup will be flowing again

Three Candles

Three candles lit their shadows cast on wall
When dancing flames make lapping circles jump
Mindful how their image can such enthrall
When watching amoeba swim in a clump

Casting light spreading out or maybe in
Darkness hiding makes blind such knowledge gained
Truth is revealed when light is cast within
Will show what once a mystery explained

Search out from rocky coast on stormy seas
The swirling beam of warning seen is bright
We can adjust our course by small degrees
On such a cold and dark and foggy night

Till morning will arrive and darkness ends
Basking in creation all life it sends

A Winter Solstice

Quiet winter, you settle into an opaque sky
You're deepest sleep in solid hues of grey
Wearing a white shroud covering a resting land
Only your scent is that of freshly fallen snow
A necklace of snow sparkle tiny diamonds
Stringed and hanging on your dark forest
Serene you glitter under dull glowing lamp
Itself burning and creating its own halo
Gone are the sounds of your scurrying feet
Walking across many crisp fallen leaves
Life now buried and alas almost forgotten
Fresh air stirs only from this sudden sound
Softly like tears flow your stream struggles
Gurgles under ice your whispering fog lifting
Along the open edges past large black stones
What little heat you seek from a fading star
Rising only slowly and now away so very far
Move away no more as far away you glide
From a summer sun that once filled the sky

White Star in Your Kiss

Softly falls a gentle snow
My love for you swirls
Lifting us in a breeze
Touching up against starlight
Making us feel alright
Reaching my tongue for you
My eyes are closed I trust
Your kiss is soft and wet
To dwell a moment just
Dissolving into my mouth
I'll take another and another
And warm your cold chill
In my precious thoughts
Let me be where you fall
There are so many now
Falling like white stars
From the black heavens
Trusting you to find me
Just knowing who you are

A Crescent Moon

Even when I wanted to hide
All what was burning inside
Under partial sky of clouds
All in my heart enshrouds
Nothing could stop its light
Searching out into the night
A beacon of forlorn hope
Searching like a telescope
To find a space to colonize
Perhaps a wave illuminate
Green and black fluorescent
Reflecting glowing crescent
Just between half and new
A reflection that it threw

Daffodazzle

Strong dark green tubes bursting through thawing ground
Higher and higher sunlight overhead
Slender your tender sheaths before me crown
Such delight awaiting the joy they spread

For so many signs of spring to espy
So very few can rightfully compare
Will Wordsworth's 'flash upon the inward eye'
Many glorious golden trumpets glare

For rite of passage in changin' seasons
Happily shove away ol' winter blues
Rightly explain and marvel more reasons
Cornucopia of chromatic hues

The happiest brightest flower of spring
For many a warm hearted smile does bring

My Angel in Scrubs

My eyes finally open
To bright lights and
Words softly spoken
No recollection
Where I am
Where I've been
Her face is aglow
Hazel eyes like smoked quartz
Blond hair halo
She speaks my name
A tender smile grows
I do the same
What a beautiful cherub
She's just like heaven
My angel in scrubs

My Woman is a Wild Flower

My woman is a wild flower
She fills my garden with grace
Lures me with her sweet fragrance
With such a brilliant radiant face
I love her long tender blossoms
On a strong leggy stem her base
Her face is made of soft petals
Her curling hair fringed lace
She is beauty from a distance
She catches my eye in every place
Up close she captures my heart
When she falls into my sweet embrace

Snowflake Kiss

Softly you fall
Drifting apart
From them all
Just one kiss
Onto my lips
Then vanishing
Ceasing to exist
Anymore because
You are gone
Never to be
Made exactly
Like that again

Index of First Lines

About the Author

This is my first attempt at publishing and distributing my own poetry that I write when I'm not duffing around on my old 1957 Allis Chalmers tractor up on my organic vegetable farm & vineyard in Alburgh Springs, VT. I reside in St. Albans, VT.